Good Ash

Good Ash

POEMS BY

KIKA DORSEY

PINYON PUBLISHING

Montrose, Colorado

Cover Art by Einat Natacha

Photograph of Kika Dorsey by Staci Bernstein

First Edition: October 2024

Pinyon Publishing
23847 V66 Trail, Montrose, CO 81403
www.pinyon-publishing.com

Library of Congress Control Number: 2024947240
ISBN: 979-8-9916083-0-5

ACKNOWLEDGEMENTS

My thanks to the editors at the following literary journals for first publishing some of the poems in this collection, though sometimes in earlier versions.

Amethyst Review: "Heaven as Cave"

Dead of Winter Anthology: "Inanna's Descent"

Gyroscope Review: "Questions from Jail"

Lothlorien Poetry Journal: "The Ditch Inside Her," "Driving in the Snow"

MacQueen's Quinterly: "After My Car Accident," "My Willow," "Skin to Skin," "Swallowtails"

Magpies: A Zoom Anthology: "Eliza, the Ravens"

Narrative Northeast: "My Virginity"

One Art: "Portrait of Katie"

Pine Row: "Origami Cranes"

Rising Phoenix Review: "If Revolutions Devolve into Terror"

Sheila-Na-Gig: "After the Storm," "I've Been Waiting Underground"

Third Wednesday Magazine: "My Father's Ghost"

We are the West: A Colorado Anthology: (Twenty Bellows): "Alchemy," "I Found Her"

Foreword

My mother was a Jungian psychologist who told me, when I was going through puberty and said I saw a squirrel the colors of the rainbow, that dreams are a sign of growth. She told me about archetypes and often of the animus, the masculine of my psyche. Many of my poems address a *you* and this is my animus, though sometimes it's to my husband I'm speaking. When I dreamed of disabled men scrambling up ladders to paint our house, she said my father's mental illness was seeping into my animus. I still dream in color. I still dream of my father, who committed suicide in a brutal way, flying headfirst out of a building from a homeless shelter on the streets of Vienna. Or my mother, who lost her memory, but in the end still expressed warmth and love and never forgot my name. They visit me in my dreams. They teach me how to fly, how to descend.

Another aspect I'm exploring in this book is the intersection between myself and the natural world. I do not see death as an end but prefer to view our bodies and consciousness as being cyclical. If hell is the underground, let's celebrate how it generates the sprouting of seeds and growth. Ash nourishes the soil.

What else that has taught me to be the spirit I am in this world is my connection to my girlfriends, my male friends, my husband, and my children. I have learned from them how to descend into the unknown, the ineffable love I feel for them and the complexity of relationship. I believe the value of literature is the intimacy it promises.

In the last section of this book, I focus on feminist themes and the bringing alive of the feminine. I have spent much of my life immersed in my body as a woman, that bleeding and curving and wondrous thing of pain and power. Our bodies are truly miraculous, as is the love of what blossoms from their breaking. I'd like to think that from my father's broken body or my mother's broken mind, something beautiful can be born, even if it's just my words. I'd like to think that my daughter will rise because of and despite our mortality, and my son will find a home that transcends any preconceived notions we've inherited through patriarchy.

I look up and see a heaven cycling into night. I look down and see my bones cycling into the light.

Contents

—PART 1—

I've Been Waiting Underground

What's a funeral barrow to one person may be a mausoleum to another,
I tell him when we light a candle called "Sea Breeze" and watch its
    fire

cackle and spit. He doesn't like the small pops and cracks of it,
hits his nerves the way the icicles drop on the dirty snow outside.

I say, *It doesn't smell like the sea,* more like mint and peony or some
    odor
that has no color of scent on our earth, this candle smelling as blue as
    his eyes.

I've been waiting underground for a swallet to come to me
and take me to the sea, and I've been to mausoleums where saints

are encrypted, their bones tucked into marble caskets.
The Pinson Mounds in Tennessee were platforms for ceremonies

above their dead, and they dug with the scapula bones of deer to
    build
the mounds of earth. My ancestors are from Tennessee. I know

its cotton and how the white bolls glow under blue skies like a sea
of white clouds. He doesn't know cotton and wants over his barrow

a candle as silent as a shy child crossing a street, following the rules
of the lights, the mother holding his hand. I want drums

resounding like the crash of waves. But I do not want sacrifice.
If I dig my grave or a mound on which to sing my song

it will be with the bones of roadkill that don't come from my car.
And now we eat our salmon and kale under yellow light and he says,

Sometimes the world seems like it's all exile and no solace,
and we read how in our city a man stabs another at Barnes and
    Noble.

My man shelved his bow and arrow in the garage. I'm burying
my mind in the candle's flame. I'm an underground away from

everyone. I've always traveled to the south of my body and I tread
lightly on this earth—its soil so generous, so noble.

Swallowtails

*We are attuned to shadows. They strafe the
shore*

   —Allen Peterson, from
   "Swallowtails"

The swallowtail has dots along its edge
a shore of yellow teardrops, of stars
against its black sea of night

and the mourning cloak turns the broken light
to a lace edge, a stripe
and I am dreaming of butterflies

while throwing coneflower seeds
onto the dark dirt patch
framing my yard

My shadow stretches its wings
weathers my shore
taste of tar and molasses

and the smelted sleep of grief
greedy for the yellow light
for the moored ship

licked by waves
that know no better
than to swallow yellow

and break it on its back
its ambit, its breadth
its warm speckled coat

to stretch winged night
along every day
without you

My Father's Ghost

1

No written ghost can rhyme, can compose music out of letters. They can't inhabit themselves with bone, but they can walk through doors, whether you open them or not.

2

My father's ghost is crowned with antlers to protect him from his manner of death, because every suicide is a predator's stalking of prey blinded by its own reflection. My father's ghost uproots a time capsule where a letter from me spells out how fawns can sleep on stone, how I have finally learned how to spell, how I promise I will not walk to the cliff's edge when the wind blows. My father's ghost surely wants me to curtail his body's drop.

3

I have my own treasure chest I never bury and rarely open. In it lies a string of pearls he gave me when I was thirty, when he said to me, *now you are surely a woman*, and leaned toward my clavicle bones and clasped the pearls around my neck. Now the skies of his gifts are blackening, so I wait out their storm to wear those scars again.

4

A ghost does not spoil children. It covers bruises with gold. It finds itself in prayer. It sheds its antlers only to adorn itself again with every memory left behind, hidden and molten like the feathers of midnight before light takes flight.

To My Body of Fifty-Eight Years

I've been a brutal blood sister to you,
with your fork-tongued reach
toward an earthen floor
that leans incessantly into
the harvest, with your womb
like a blind eye of a hermit
banished to a cave and then
brought out carrying the gods
they created. Yes, you fashioned
what was holy out of serpents,
salt, and the starlight of desire.
You've made me crave everything
that killed me—bourbon,
the sweet taste of tobacco,
the feel of a bucking horse
between your legs. You lacked
fortitude when I gained it
and you accrued power
when I lost every door to a waning
light I had to catch to save
the ones I love, to lend them
our milk or the strength of our palms,
so you took our hands and we punched
through walls other bodies built.
My neck strains from the city
of my heart; my navel flowers
like the released prisoner it is.
I am so cursed with you
that I am blessed, and I carry
you with the grace
of a burning torch in the wind.

Driving in the Snow

It makes me think
of Indiana
and lake-effect storms
of learning how to pump
brakes ahead of time
how to turn and lift your foot
from the gas pedal
and feel your back end
slide into the turn

I had a dream that my car
was a bull I was riding
with horns spiking
a wide blue sky
We were careening downhill
and it was always November
the time of the slaughter
I was going to go home
to tell my lover
that a fence was down

You see,
no love of mine
has sufficient fencing
but at least the cattle
can roam free
and we have to give
the sacrificed
another chance
I mean, we concocted
a whole religion out of it

Now I'm driving on ice
and I can skid
buck and spin
I can crawl slowly
and I can tell you
that the slaughter
is long over
the freezer packed with meat

We're right in the center
of winter's cross
riding a bull
playing with the edge
its rotten pickets
coiled barbed wire
dust packed and frozen
ropes untied
the road a long shadow

and you in the cold sun

While You Calculate a Reason to Live

The horses are coming in. They gallop across the plains while you
calculate a reason to live. They know in the barn

are stalls with troughs kindness will fill with grain when the bell
rings, when the sun sinks, and you know that very fire of it

you worshipped when it was in your loins, when it warmed the
    blocks
of coal you wrapped in newspaper to make it last longer, scribbled
    with

news full of tragedy, and that was what youth was—carrying the
    world
not only despite its faults but because of how it held heat, its hell-fire

keeping you warm, you felling trees to build a barn for the horses,
which now bend and touch your palm with their velvet noses.

Something scared you once—a danger far away. A flood. A long-held,
ominous silence. A curvature of space. A geometry of time where the
    future

revealed itself in a pulled card of an old man blinded, stumbling with
    a cane.
The horses brought relief. You curried their coats like burnishing a
    coin.

You watched the kind of light you will believe, a signal you can still
    make
with your own hands crunching paper with so many stories,

while a whole country aims to put out fires, the horses bend
their necks toward grain they ignited with hunger, and you

calculate a reason to live, time on your tongue like a folding
promise of future, and the sun rolls on its back, threshing its light.

The Dissonant Music of Memory

I am weary of being the stories I tell about myself,
the one of Miller moths taking over the city and crowding

with their dusty wings around our yellow kitchen light,
the one of my father overdosing and passed out in a cornfield

in Indiana. I do not know if this is true. I just saw the firetruck
and police car on that hot Midwestern day and fed my sister

a fried bologna sandwich. But it may have been chocolate ice cream.
Maybe they found my father in a warehouse behind the pizza

restaurant the mafia owned, with its illegal smokers where
I used to drink tepid beer and play Blackjack. Or they found him

on the grounds of Notre Dame near the pond where I swam, and
fish kissed me, and it was dark, the moon hidden behind clouds.

I am weary of concocting lives and etching a self out of the black
    charcoal
of my ignorance, of excavating tools with my bare hands,

then chiseling bone into effigies of haloed saints, their hands clasped
in prayer for me, and I am ever so weary of me.

My father was a good man and he was not a good man.
I think we can say that about everyone.

I did learn Blackjack and my luck was as fickle as the stem
of an autumn leaf, and I always risked losing instead of giving up.

My father played me dissonant music on the piano.
My sister is a moth seeking a flame that is not too hot,

and I pray below the minor notes of my light that the ending of the
    story
will resolve, that the protagonist who is me will gently disappear in
    the dark.

The Crack We Can't Step On

Heaven's infinity must surely contain
teardrops and the finitude of dried leaves,
of autumn's exhausted sigh
in its vaulted cathedral.

I imagine my mother in that heaven
crocheting the rhythm that blankets my mind
when I pull the sheets over my nakedness,
where I cluck that rhythm with my tongue,
rap my hand on my thigh,
the staccato beat like predictable sidewalk cracks,
my mother slithering through them,
my father in a field of lavender counting pills
and swallowing the exact right dose,
me skydiving in a vast expanse of blue
over fields promising a harvest,
where gravity is an acrobat
plunging me upwards
into a crack in the sky,
my back released from the burden
of flimsy sails that are supposed to save me,
released from that crescendo
where all we can see on the horizon
is the fall,
that crack I see between a swath of grassland
and the open sky,
even though its breach we never could step on
even if we tried to,

as it recedes like sirens
into the night.

Heaven as Cave

You need to make redemption
out of your dust and bones
as you knot melodies in your hands
that reach for the child,
scarred and full of healing,
the child made of the shadow plays
in your cave.

I never believed in anything
but heaven as a cave
with stalactites reaching
from the ceiling
and the water as still
as my father's eyes on God,
the bats as dark as their home,
heaven an underground heart
encased in ribs of contrition,
and my mother a reservoir of memory,
a water where I steer my canoe
to the cave's opening,
shaft of light the belief
that her wounded mind could heal
in the dark water.

Verticality promised stars for homes
but I only knew how to scaffold
from the wood of fallen trees
and when I rose higher

than my outstretched arm
I could see how the devil
lived in cloud and sun
and I buried my God
and I chose to believe
that not all ghosts rise.
They dig through the earth
with the scapular bones
of timid and gentle deer
and fill our graves
with jewels and arrows.

My father saddles my horse,
my mother kneads my dough,
my lover lives as long
as horizons on the plains
where underground
is a treasure we cannot see yet,
and the children collect stones,
every one of them a promise.

Questions from Jail

Have you seen the shriveled grass near the jail?
Did you step carefully to avoid the rattlers?
Did you try to get past the guards to see me?
How many broken mouths can they carry?
How can their voice taste like such disdain?
How did the homeless woman in the cell
run like a forgotten river in a gutter?
Will her meth-eaten teeth ever be replaced?
Do you know that for every person in jail,
there's a beetle carrying you across drought-ridden land?
Did you know that for all shining badges
you have given up your bloody heart,
have holstered light against the shadow of ashes
that is you?
Did you know that you planted yourself
with the sole of a giant boot,
while in the jail someone vomits
canned beef and soggy green beans?
Did you expect someone else to fix the broken well
or sell you flowers instead of the bouquet of blades
I hugged to me and called memory and regret
as I watched *Ellen* on the tiny TV, headphones on,
orange jumpsuit like a uniform for a war
I never wanted to fight?
Would you like to piss in front of a probation officer
with red stringy hair and a tattoo
of a winding snake on her arm?
Did you know baby rattlers are more dangerous

than adults because they can't control their venom?
Can you see how young I was in all
the happening, departing, claiming, and rootlessness
of the war of growth?
Will you call that a crime?
Did you know that dung beetles navigate
by the Milky Way and not the sun or moon?
Have you ever seen the sky from a jail cell
with its bars and outside the boundless expanse
of a midnight you can call your own?
Can you see the trail of light,
the shit-laden beetles,
the gavel like a clapper of a bell,
the sweaty neck of a lover,
the judges of paradise promising to bring you home
down the long road in hell,
how the air sometimes tastes like baby pine,
how your roadside blue sky is so hot, so dry,
how to return home is like that first thirst
you have ever known,
the naked skies like a feast?

Hell, Michigan

Maybe the neighbors in Hell
care about each other
at the racetrack and tavern,
at the pool and in the kitchens,
lying underneath quilts,
in the devil-breath
of small-town comfort.
Here in the city I concoct stories
out of people I only see on buses,
driving toward some heaven
I imagine in the grid splattered
like stars on a map, on a flag.

There are different reasons hell is Hell.
Those blood-sucking insects.
Strangling forest.
Wetlands where your feet sink.
Mothers who yell at their drunk husbands,
"He's gone to hell!"
Reeves, the patriarch and founder, saying,
"What the hell, call it anything."
The German immigrants saying it's "hell,"
which means *bright.*
Bright as the horse that won that race,
as the glint of whiskey in the sun,
as Michigan I knew as a child,
where the forests drank me
and the beech trees clothed in moss

pillowed my dreams.
I've learned in my old age to return there
when I sleep.
I return to how the forests tucked me in.
I return to the winds that tore its branches.
Strangers gathered the broken wood
and built a park.

I want to go where the devil
tells me my dreams
are the nightmares
that do not drown the bright rays
of their making.
The sex pillowed on green grass.
The pond's filthy algae feeding the ducks.
The lies we tell to protect.
Where I can love
in the sin of tucking and raking
all that has fallen.
All that hell-spent
detritus that is all we have given
or mistaken.
When a forest was cleared
for a small town and we invited even
those we did not love.
Even the strangers
swimming in the mill pond,
their children
skulling and skimming
across the algae, above minnows,
in the shallow end.

We show the children
the long summers in hell,
how we sweat with their growing
and striving and dying,
and Hell bellies up to us
in its green waters.
It's our lovely damnation
of loving without
a compass of morality,
our bodies tucked in the dark forest
while we dive in the deep.

—PART 2—

Dreaming

I've not read the news in two days so I am dreaming
about lakes so cold I can't swim in them.

My father beckons to me on shore, and it is dark.
I am dreaming of a hybrid car I think I own

but have to return after I try to seduce the driver,
who is a veteran and crippled from a war.

I do not know what war.
It could be the one in Ukraine, or Ethiopia, or Yemen,

and all I know is how breathing comes so easily,
like the way the injured man slides his leg

and it arcs before planting like the curve of a planet,
and I realize I don't own the car so I will return it,

and my father reaches out for me and touches my hand,
saying, *swim*, and I'm looking at the cold water

and bracing myself, holding my breath and pulling
my hair off my face, the wet strands from my cold sweat,

the water dark with ripples of white lines in the moonlight,
my father asking from me what is not impossible but difficult,

the wars trudging forward, the motors of the world spent
on oil I will never own, and I with my broken hesitation

to plunge into the place where the light is darkest.
I lift my head when I hear words that have not been written

while noticing the crickets stopped singing this late autumn day,
have buried pupa underground where they sing in their sleep.

My Willow

My willow, like me,
has turned every sentence into questions,
older now, with four trunks leaning and torn,
propped up with a wedge of wood
to save the bees living in its hollow.
It wonders how the canopy can touch ground,
how to collapse toward root.

It is your silence, love,
how the bark with lines
enter us in our own canopy,
lines like wind-roads
into this neighborhood
of not knowing,
though we hold it in our memory
like its shade,
like its tire swing shaped like a horse
we've given away to children,
or the tree house we took down,
nails jammed into it dislodged.
We sawed off the branches,
brittle and precarious and leaning
into our safe street.

Its forgiveness stood so close to me.
Touched me.

The arborist wants to cut it down.
But the bees, we say,
and the branches that still sprout
their thin green leaves,
waving in the breeze.

I do not know what to confess to it.
Surely, I long to age with so much grace,
honey in my hollows,
a question on my tongue
that helps me listen to the wind.

The Wind is a Pauper

The wind is a pauper planning a revolution, a falling
of willow branch, fence slat, nails, and broken buds of spring.

I meant to dream of us running for the bus on the street
next to the pasture, how we shout each other's names

in the din of the wind, how we anticipate shelter
and wheels below us, how we have somewhere to go,

but instead I lay in bed awake listening to whispering
after I held our dog while he seized and died, and you said,

It was the wind, and I said, *No, it was something else,*
but I couldn't make out any words. Then you left

and I stayed in our home feeling his absence while the wind
knocked and groaned, and outside the willow bowed in the dark.

The wind promises me new regimes where doors open to the buds
that blind us in their light, where *hush* becomes *husk* peeled

to reveal kernels for the horses that lean over the fence
so we can feed them while we wait for the bus

in the dream I never had. You see, I miss you, and I miss
the soft black and white fur of our dog. I could tell

how heavy he was in your arms, how you struggled
with his dead weight. And now the king and queen have fallen

and I feel their empty thrones in my spine and neck,
the ache of all we left behind, while the pauper gathers

fallen branches and promises us this revolution will not devolve into
    terror.
The horses in the dream I never had crane their necks toward me

like an answer. The bus windows are dark. A whisper asks me
to hush and listen. A May crown topples in the light.

After the Storm

The water is always turbid after a storm, I tell him,
and he is ironing a blue tie with yellow butterflies.

Outside the sun slants and cuts across the river's surface.
Three daughters are setting three birds on the globe.

We will go where they land, the youngest says.
Somewhere are insurrections, the Midwest cornfields

flattened by tornadoes, somewhere is a bitter taste
like coffee grounds and ash on our tongues,

and I think of the day the river was transparent. He and I
caught trout with a fly and fried them with rosemary and lemon.

We always fed the children first because the future left our bodies
long ago, when the butterflies found milkweed faster

than we could run, when the daughters learned how to feed
the birds, to not give them too much millet, to mix

their water with apple cider vinegar. They learned to take care.
And now the storm is rolling by another home. A roof shivers.

A barn pushes back. The horses stand with their rumps to the wind.
Some Pavlovian moment makes me want to go into the basement

and wait out the storm, but I stay above ground, and what we unbury
can fly, what topples can burst into color, and the birds are perched

on the jigsaw countries I've never seen. I look out the window
at the murky river. A shaft of sun slices like a wing across its current.

The water snags against stone and sings its plaintive song,
and I think of my love, how like this it is—slicing, snagging, singing.

Alchemy

1

She has trodden on trails made of granite and gold, of an alchemy that the sting of summer promised when she was thriving in the hive, drinking honey with it. Across the Atlantic a war touched all her shadows, and the ghosts of three women pleated her hair. It was the color of rust.

2

She had two children but always dreamed of a third, another daughter whose wind she could give her blood to. Her mother once told her she would never, in the midnight sun of pregnancy, be able to afford what she could beget. As if wrists don't bend. As if money were palmed by wombs.

3

She watched summer hold her daughter's hand. The war traced all its truths, stamping nationality onto its coins of night, the refugees like sacrificial lambs stirring soup in Moldova, sleeping in subways. Her daughter found her own three fates in the heavy goblet of sky. Drank from it. Said, *Mom, in one you're not there.*

4

To change granite to gold you need lemon juice, rosemary, urine, gravel, salt, bourbon, and honey. You need to change your name. You need to erase the face on the coin, watch it dissolve, and then flip it and know there is nothing to call except the summer light—a coaxing, a red-rust dawn.

Gods of the North

I never knew anything of winters anywhere but in the north,
the Rust Belt in Indiana, where the snow would turn black with

soot but the push and lean of the St. Joe River kept its green waters
from freezing. As a child I waited for summers when I could walk

on railroad tracks to Potawatomi's park. The oak trees had leaves
as big as hands. I lay in their shade on patches of grass, dandelion,

dirt, and onion grass I sucked the root of. Everything tessellated like
that grass in my life, patches polygons of every color made of

my sweat and the dreams fringing my edges of escape. I stitched
leaf, snow, and cement into the curtain of a god's lustrous hair,

how it fell gracefully over the shoulders of a giant's industry—
the Studebaker factory closed, downtown with boarded-up

shacks of broken businesses, and the river's promise a lantern
born of a fiery curse. It shined for me. Its movement was

a stitch, a brush, a mending of all that had been cut—
my family's difficult love, my youth. I believed

in the river. I believed it knew where it was going
but kept it a secret. I strolled on railroad ties and to a tree

that promised me it held that river's secret in its veins,
while the loud and spoken gods of the North came from a myth

where they die in the end, collapse into ash. I never meant
to tell that story again so I gathered only what came

from listening to the swoosh and slide of water, the words
you may regret, the crane's motor grumbling as it built

one concrete slab or brick at a time, with windows riddled
across the wall's side. I looked through their transparency

at the geometry of my life. Shapes of every love and loss.
Skyscraper silos. Husked corn. Curtains of cloud. Taste

of steel and ethanol. I saw all the words. Heard the color.
Joined it all together into a collage, an alchemy, and found a home

where there was none, found a god where the heavens
collapsed and fell on me like rain.

Prayer

I haven't a way to climb past the dry seasons
into your arms, the way they rain and drop

from heavens that never answered my questions.
The pond is sinking like the nights, and the breath

of a day lends wind to the blackbird wings, while
my hands are empty of joy and all I thought was mine.

You are behind me like a twisted road and reach before me
like an invisible season, one born out of the grace

of burying, of folded wings and autumn's waning light.
In my shadow I sometimes see you,

how you etch me with the dark. Behind me is
yellow corn, before me a harvest to feed the cattle,

a slaughter in November, a child a child
no more, a place where her first words

get lost in the clatter of all that followed them.
I wonder what their sound was, whether

you lent them your accent, your foreign lilt, your remnant
from a home we all see as other, outside the dry ditch,

the prairie aster, our bones, someplace of origin's spoken need.
Sometimes now I hear how what you have left behind is

full of asking, both questions and demands,
or more like a pleading not to move the target

or lock the door, to cool this hot planet so that
we don't burn, to come to us in the silence.

If Revolutions Devolve into Terror

If so, and the night washes us of our collective mind, why do the
     crows
know to stay together on the oak tree in the winter, terror the ice
     enshrining

its bare branches, roadkill on the street they share, bats overhead
swooping so fast that only an individual mind can perceive them

while crows sleep together but we never see their bodies in the dark,
black feather against black night? I asked you about Kant's

categorical imperative, to act in accordance with rules that can
hold for everyone. I said, *This is how I try to live, as long as the rules*

demand kindness and not supplication to authority. Outside an old
     man
in a wheelchair rolls on ice toward the door of the dentist office

and I hold it open for him. But at night sometimes the guillotine
     falls
when I dream of driving in the snow and not checking my speed,

running into the oak tree and you with your big hands on your eyes,
weeping in the passenger seat. I've never known equanimity

except when my ideals settled in my hips or grew lush long before
the harvest, maybe without it; maybe the stalks of corn tip

and enter the soil like the romantic power of imagination or
the transcendence without the abstract ideal to name it, consume it.

When we give up the road to understanding we cease to see the world,
housing our fears of the unknown in oak trees that grow so familiar,

satellites becoming our celestial bodies. Yet God is written outside of
    Reason
and a niggling feeling that all you have done has been worth it,

even the devolutions that taught you reason's limitations.
I have found a home. I have learned the crow's detachment

from any symbol in its murder, and I have driven to a madness
where we should all at some point go. The amber light of exhaust and
    sunset,

the stretching light waves, set my body on fire, and the crows,
balancing on a patina of ice, drink the light and do not give it back.

—PART 3—

To My Animus

You can be infinity
and I an American wife.
We can wrestle in my dreams
where I bandage your wounds
and begrudge the days
of binding what is broken.

You ask me to save
every coin you minted.
You are the color of a sandstorm
in the Arizona desert,
welded and hot,
unsheathed in the dark.
We are the color
of the middle of my heart.
You mark the way to it.
I pay for entrance.

My life is a dwarf star
and you the warm map
of my constellation.
I set infants on my lap
and you legislate.
I am snow
and you plow.
It snows every spring
and the angels give God
the silent treatment.
I listen to its emptiness.
I sing lullabies.

You're doubling in Cartesian formulas.
Two rings: engagement and marriage.
Golden and promising.
One welded from the coins
the color of Arizona sandstorms.
One embedded with its passing.

I'd like to go to that desert,
watch the antelope wait
out the torrential wind,
how their cloven hooves
are like you and me,
tilling the earth,
our bodies a witching rod,
underneath us the sea.

Surrender

The desert is nothingness, my lover says, and I am splaying out
my bloody hands palms-up to a blue sky pressing down

on sand, sage, cacti, and barbed-wire fences. Our green car
is parked next to a cholla while on the dashboard is the cactus's

skeleton pocketed with lacy holes and hollow as this sky, as
the space between my fingers ringed with silver and crystal.

The desert is an open skirt weaving blossoms above needles.
The desert hurts. I bloom my hands into his, our love nothing

like the wound of the sun I fisted when lonely, nothing
like the November slaughter behind us or the Christmas blur

of birth before us, nothing but the folding of seasonless landscapes
like memories. In one I cupped his shoulder beneath a trellis

of thorny wild roses and the door of the dry desert swung open
to reveal a creek bed with water gurgling on volcanic black stone.

We bent to drink what the skin of the land had sweated for us,
when we were young and in love and a tiny golden band

fit on my finger. Now I rinse the blood from my hands. Beneath
its red glare the flesh is the color of the wild antelope blending

with the sand, the cholla surrendering as all weaponed things
eventually do, its tips of yellow flowers stretching, and I say,

See, this is something. On the horizon, no matter how hard the sky
tries here, it cannot be soft. Its line not errant. Its smell like

copper and sage. Its promise spooning the moon. The tips of my finge
tingle like the blue kiss of stars. Before us the land clings to the sky.

The Bones

I'll tell you a secret.
My husband was roasting chicken
and my children were in the center
of the kitchen arguing about how
all the grandfathers of the world
were stupid, were bringing them down
with their yachts and votes and all their
smoke-belching magic.
The moon was white as paper
smudged with the gray of charcoal
by a divine artist trying to sketch what is naked,
how the hip smears into the world.
We were roasting that bird
and the bones were doing what bones do—
pushing us out of sight into night and darkness
and the white of what that dark becomes,
setting us into the sun that burns,
giving us a taste of leg and wing.

We were there in the kitchen
and I didn't tell them how I had lifted my mother's
urn from the shelf, beside the deer skull
and prairie dog spine, opened it, dipped my hand
into the crumbled gray, and tasted her ashes.
They were gritty with her bone.
They were bitter and sweet.
While my son and daughter were digging
their own mysterious dirt,
I was trying to evolve,
tasting bone.

I've been riding a junk boat into my thoughts.
It's a small canoe on the edge of ditch.
That's where I find those sickle bones.
I've been eating ash and bones
and I've been loving the deer
that curve their necks toward my apples,
the prairie dogs who burrow into the earth
and then give back what they have taken
from their dark underworld.
I have carried harvests and feasts
on my back in a world of hunger,
how they give me back all that is lost,
ashen like the disciple
of the moon.

After My Car Accident

1

Autumn rain collects in our leaf-filled gutters and drips on the grill. The rhythm of it is faster than my heart, each beat of the water's drum defying any dissonance the rain could create like during the flood ten years ago, which turned our streets to rivers. I listen to its *drip, drop, drip, drop,* and I am a kind mind, a living mind; I allow the rain to have its way.

2

I was in a car accident and now loud sounds make me jump. Do you know the smell of airbags when they deploy and tear with your weight? It's a chemical smell. The car fills with smoke as it spins. Now I am alone with the rain and my bruises.

I don't think I'll ever be surprised again. I don't think, *job, light, fire, blood.* I don't let my body come out.

3

My son says he is dissecting cadavers for school. I imagine the boy I gave birth to, how he was purple with the effort to travel through me, how this boy now had to witness so much death. But there is always poetry when we look at how we muscle through the world and build our homes. The paint cracks, some remedies are poisonous, the guilty party doesn't confess, the façade falls, the river breaks through its banks, and it never stops raining. But I know my son has a roof over his head. I know he can plant his feet on this spinning earth.

4

Most people will not be your friend. Most water will not freeze. Most snowflakes will melt. Your blood will travel mostly in your body, even if you bleed. The future is a dim light. You say you don't want to go. You say you haven't packed and the dog needs you. You say, *job, dark, ice, stop spinning, stop spinning.* Outside the heart of the world is beating anyway, telling you to move on.

Winged

I miss the birds, I tell him, as a shaft of morning light
releases from a crystal, rainbows crashing against the wall.

In February, even the blackbirds don't sing on the cattails,
the woodpecker doesn't hammer our roof, mourning doves

and robins don't swoop or hop in our backyard's dry dirt.
The parakeets we once kept in a golden cage have died,

their ashes mingling on the slope of Bear Mountain.
I can't feel flight, I continue. He is a silent landing.

He is forgetting the boy of the sky, the one who dived off cliffs.
He is a long road clinging to a canyon with walls

only the mountain sheep know as well as I my own feet,
with their clinging tendons, how tired they are.

I reach to touch my shoulders, ache for wings. Outside it snows.
One bird was green with a blue tailfeather. He would hop

on my fingers, ride my shoulders as I cooked. Now I gaze
out the window where a hawk rides the wind.

Some seasons only the predators survive, and the prisms
are the promise of capturing light like a song its meandering notes.

I'm hungry, listening, but wary of hunts. The hawk dives.
The slaughter is not on February's calendar, just the aching empty
   belly.

I would fly to rainforests, I say. *Hot jungle. Winged dirges of song,*
canopy calling me. But now all I remember is the girl I was,

all the springs that found me risen.

Origami Cranes

We can find the origami cranes everywhere in the papers of our
    youth,
the way we folded and loved, the way now in the spring

we drive through mountain passes to valleys—the Arkansas to San
    Luis—
to find the cranes returning to the north. They descend on fields

of sage, their legs sunk in snowmelt mud, their wings long and thin
like willow leaves. But it's February now, the month of hearts

and chocolate, of flight postponed until spring, buried beneath
    blankets,
and migration a hope, a fleeting thought, a leaning of flower

against bud, breast against pillow, while children cut hearts from
the very paper cranes used to arrive from. They give them freely

to their friends at school. They walk on buckled sidewalks
with a bag full of valentines, and on the horizon socked-in smog

reddens the sinking sun. It spreads our fire toward the low ground
while we listen for the clattering sound of the cranes in our minds

and our hearts fold and fold, the wind winnows its way
through snowmelt, the chaff our threshed love,

the children perching hopeful on our breasts.

I have chosen spring more times than I can remember.

I've unfolded my pelvis to birth what the seed of love planted.
I've spent February feeding cranes in my dreams,

the wheat that was supposed to grow in a country riddled by war.
I have told you this: cranes look fragile with their long legs,

their beaks like knives separating grain from chaff,
but they know, like my love, to always return.

As I do. Even when there is too much between us.
Even when it snows in spring and all that melts is the shape of clouds.

Good Ash

When I give my son a night light
with chickadees and vines
when this life I buried with words
a staggering bonding
of trinities
whether they are gods or families
I have arrived in a new year

I have braided flags with dissent
I have fed the birds millet in the dark
I have pinned to the wind every ghost that haunts me
They were on fire with my love

Sometimes I hold close to my chest
all the asking
the morning chorus
the small change
the not wanting to do harm
mines, borders, cigarettes
coyotes caught in barbed wire
my handful of copper and silver
a mountain demanding my ice
a window shut to the cold

Carry me exactly here and I will carry you
Let's look at how we shift
like the hollow bones of birds
poised for flight

I saw our first hunger
how time assuaged all of it

In the gutter I was generous.
In my home I saved
the good ash
gave it a future

Even the silent hunting hawk
broke into song

—PART 4—

Skin to Skin

I was a dust mote.
Because of you, I am a mountain.
                    —Rumi

1

It never was my intention to float lazily through the living room, reflecting the light, unsure where I would land. I was shed from your skin, that kind of Eve, not even granted the rib of bone. I spent years unable to vote, years toiling in kitchens to feed what fueled your power. Now I angle toward the corner of the room where the spider webs me a mountain.

2

The creation of the world comes from weaving hands, the spider-like three Fates, and even though I share your skin I am not you. It's all just sex and shedding, birth and loss, mountains and the flat plains like my palms over our babies' bellies. Not even centuries now I've voted. I've cast ballots and nets and gathered seeds. I've climbed my peak to watch you enter a mine. Breathe in coal dust.

3

It never was my intention to sweep myself into a dustpan and release me into the elements. But I did. Winter threatens and a regime is on the verge of collapse. There are wars. You have angled north and all the spiders move inside. They know how to stay above ground, how to corner their universe. I've found in my legs an anchor from which I can rise and look down. The city lights you up in the dark.

Phantom Pain

The sisters move in tandem across a field of sage and I am
witnessing the dance I always joined, where they sashay across a
    desert floor

prophesizing peace, passive as print, while a mushroom cloud billows
its way up to God, a MacBeth of a bomb. Lady Macbeth mourned
    the child

she lost, who suckled on her breast like a calf. The bomb was revenge
but the innocent died, and my sisters say they don't believe in
    revenge.

They want to lie on the sand and welcome radioactive light into their
    graves.
My son tells me that morality is relative and I ask, *Is it, really?*

I do not even know my own hands. I suspect he may be right. I
    would
kill if it saved his life. Yet I have never lost a child. I have never
    experienced a land at war.

The battle I feel is the ache of old injuries and wondering
what I could have done to avoid them, what I could have done
    better to heal.

I know little of healing. I do not even know why my father's suicide
    resides
in the ladder of my ribs where he climbs and jumps headfirst again
    and again.

You see, life is hard and there are different kinds of battles. I believe love
can be as solid as bone. I love my sisters, one freckled like a speckled

valley of wildflowers, one carving her name on all the fallen timber
we feel in our legs as we grow older, as our children never levitate

and pray fervently for a still earth. They do not ask permission
for this life we've given them, for the quench

of their own panging pain of thirst. They do not take for granted
that the sun will fall gently, that it will land on its feet, free of pain.

I'm Always Turning Around

In the dream, I drive up into the mountains with my mother, and we need to turn around, but first I pull over to a view of the city. It's a collage of pipes and buildings, bathed in light, glowing blue and silver, full of curves and lines like the painting of a city I gave to my mother as a child. I gaze at it and hold her hand, and I know we have to return, drive the curvy roads along pine and spruce where the bears forage, the mountain lions hunt, and the pinecones fall.

Did I ever tell you how much I miss my mother? Did I ever tell you how she painted portraits, and I cities; she faces, and I buildings? If you merged our work, you would have to ask my sister for the landscapes. Then we would see something complete.

I have never felt complete. I have lost those I loved and I have lost my way in the woods until I descended to a fishery, boxed-in streams of trout in the mountains, rows of them, and the building with a tin roof and a man smoking in front of it. He took me home in a truck. I thought of the fish, how small their home.

I have lost so much and sometimes I fear I'll lose you.

In the dream I know I'll turn around. I always return to my home with pipes like intestines and you pounding chicken to make cordon blue, to my children who are about to leave us, to our dog sprawled on the red Oriental rug. I always return, carrying the city in my eyes—I in my black boots waiting tables, men with their jackhammers, children emptying brick schools. I return with the mountains on my shoulders and the faces of my family, eyes hooded with melancholy or as bright as light on water.

They look right at you through the paint's oil, and my sister is always moving, looking for new landscapes. She seeks the succulent sea of the South, the cypress with their root-legs, the prairies with their barns. I just know mountains. That's where I found you. That's where I'm always turning around. And you are home and you are not home and our lines are as tenuous as an autumn rain, as the brush of paint on a canvas once so open, so empty, so past, so complete without us.

Sunyi

1

I don't know if Sunyi was her name, the word in Indonesian for *solitary*, but I do remember it started with an s. She was a skinny orangutan who was stuck on a piece of land when the black river rose in Kalimantan, in the jungle where we researched her kind with Birute, the Jane Goodall of that lesser-known ape. Birute didn't want to rescue Sunyi right away because she was the worst thief of them all, stealing our clothes and stringing them from trees. We needed a break from her antics. After a week Sunyi ran out of fruit, the river sank, she came back, and she grabbed my hand on the pier as I fed her pineapple. She placed my hand on her forehead and made the sound of weeping. Sunyi, I realized, had been lonely.

2

Orangutans are known to be the solitary apes. When you try to teach them sign language, they throw down your hands and shake their heads. But Sunyi was like me. I steal from lives while I eavesdrop in hot tubs and scribble conversations in my lonely office. I caress, I sex, I decorate trees, I grasp hands of lovers I later throw down. I am not orange like fruit but the color of rust—the wearing away of self from loneliness or another's needs, chapped tits and empty days all tangled up in the paradox of my life.

3

Rusty bodies in my western world are train cars covered in graffiti, their plaintive whistles both lulling me to sleep and keeping me up. I had a mother who did the same, a father who did nothing but gave me a reason for her lullabies. I wonder if Sunyi slept on that fruit tree as she slowly denuded it of its lonely promise. I remember the feeling of her hand, how thick her dark skin, calloused from climbing, rough against mine, her brown eyes meeting mine like dark paint spattered on a journey I had taken to find her and a journey I would take to leave her, alone in that jungle and rescued not by humanity, not by anything other than the vicissitudes of time and the way everything sinks like a head into a pillow, again and again, so we can walk, hungry, across a bridge to shore.

Inanna's Descent

I never wanted to be a witch for Halloween,
just her black cat that clawed at summer skies
till the Midwestern autumn opened,
dropped its red and yellow paint on leaves.
I never wanted to be the ghost but the cowgirl,
riding through Michigan's cornfields
dodging bullets from the mad farmer
while summer's fat burned off toward bone.

I had no gripe with the seasons gods doled out to me,
saw them as another saw to the wood,
fire to the tinder,
mother to the wound.
I was never the Sumerian Inanna,
just her descent with walls of limestone and salt
and effigies lined on their shelves.
I stripped all seven garments off me into days
with no day of rest, naked
when the seven judges struck me dead.

I never loved my sister,
Queen of the Underworld,
just her necklace of stars,
and I never meant for my lover to follow me,
to break off the phallic stalagmites
to fashion weapons for a war he couldn't win.
Where our sex was released is where
I learned to climb,

my lover doomed half the year to the underworld,
my dead self alive once again.
He had to create that winter.
He dressed himself in wolf and jackal hides
and an uncanny failed attempt to embrace
an unconditional love I never asked for, or gave
to anyone but my children.

And yet I never wanted anything but him,
anything but his release from that dark cave
I wanted to claim as mine, mine only,
so the summer, tumbling
like a cat off a witch's broom,
like the mad farmer's hat in the wind,
again and again,
can break into bloom.

My Virginity

My virginity
was a hole my Catholic mother dug
in our garden
a paradise the always summer
and my virginity
with crumbled dirt on its edges
my mother with her iron shovel
of God
and I grafting apple trees
and planting them
while she watered me
with holy water

My virginity was her labor of love
while I pocketed the coins
I stole from her antique desk
to buy something sweet
chocolate smooth as a baby's palm
something sweet for me alone
and she forever in the garden
trying to make something out of me
by making me fence the bed
from the rabbits
who can fuck all day

flimsy fence
with no barbs
because my mother loved me
too much
to make me threaten blood

She wore a red hat
with a wide brim
and a golden cross
and she kept digging
and I with my lightning clit
and I with my empty womb
was doomed to disappoint

oh, Mother,
the days were so long then
the soil so fertile
even the worms couldn't sleep
and when the foxes died of mange
there were too many rabbits

They hopped about the periphery of the fence
they were as foolish as I
thinking every day
might be their last
and our lazy dog
just rolled in the grass

She liked to feel
how dense the green grows
supine on her back
open to the strong muscle of sun
empty sky begging for its light
and getting all of it
every piercing beam
bees droning in the lavender
crickets rising from the ground, singing
and that animal body
also rolling
in every shadow
my hunger cast

Eliza, the Ravens

We drive on forgotten highways
through the desert of California,
halt at a rest stop
where a flock of ravens caws at us
and the saguaros reach toward the smoky sky.
I think how I should have stopped in Vegas
and turned aces to gold for you, my daughter.
I wonder what your new home will look like,
whether it will be as busy as our rug of temples and flowers.
I hope it will be less red.
I hope it has cool colors.

You don't remember the pattern of your birth.
That's what mothers do,
carry the refracted light of your entrance to this—
cacti and the coast with a blue boat—
while you are crystal throwing out prisms
and the clouds don't know where they're going,
and sometimes they blanket the rays like a mother.

At home your father catches spiders
and throws them into the grass.
Your brother coils ropes for future climbs.
At home the ditch is full of water
and the cards are in a drawer.

I stopped gambling when I lost sight
of what winning looked like.

Here we watch a man
in a shirt with an image of an alligator drinking beer.
He throws the crust of his sandwich to the ravens
and they argue about who will eat it.
One of them snatches it, gulps it down.

There is always one winner
while the rest of us turn away
and hop on the dust,
maybe fly.

Portrait of Katie

She sits with buried head,
won't look into your eyes,
a woman who bled in prisons,
who spent nine years locked up
for a bag of pot and some pills,
mocked by a cruel cellmate,
begging the guards to see a doctor.
Eventually, after vomiting
the canned beans they forced her
to eat, doubled up on the cold
linoleum, they sent her to a doctor,
who removed her entire colon.

She smells like stale cigarettes,
her bleached hair now dyed auburn.
I want to touch it.
It looks so soft, shiny and copper
like a new penny,
her thin shoulders caressed by it.
Her lover of twenty-seven years
just died and now she holds
his memory tight against her, filled
with shadow and color, her past
a long highway that led
to a place she couldn't leave,
her future a gutted fish,
a waterfall pressing her shoulders,
a stage where the red boat

may find that water tucked
between the fall
and the stone
and rest for a bit,
listening to the roar.

The Ditch Inside Her

She felt she should be grateful
she didn't have to walk
across the two-by-four bridge,
the ditch dry.
She could scramble down
its bank, cross it to
the grassy plains,
yellow with winter and drought.

But in the ditch was
the red scab of dried algae,
discarded plastic bottles,
and a tiny baby shoe
torn by the water and weathering,
with gray braided laces
and a frayed sole.
The gray may have been
blue beneath its dust.

What child walked barefoot
where the spiky yucca pierces?
What child are we missing
from the laconic ditch's stories?

We have missed her for far too long.
Her hair fell into its water
in the summer, and the crown vetch
grew ravenous near the shore,
and there was no war to fear.

She walks across the plank
regardless of the dry ground
offering what is easy.
She is working on her balance,
and she is caught
in all its damming
and all its release—
barefoot, ruined,
gray as rain.

The Daughters

The daughters open their hands to rain.
They wrap November and give it to God.
The daughters take our future
and sprinkle lavender oil
to calm the angry storms.
The daughters run with dogs.
They paddle kayaks in rapids.
They learn karate.
They leave their homes
and build their own
with the stone of mountains,
with windows forged from sea glass,
with every day they lifted themselves
from the dust, palms pressing
the arena's floor,
the horse bucking beside them,
then still as cloud
on a day of no wind
and the daughters know how to gentle,
how to weave wind from their dance.

The daughters dream you
out of autumn's grave.
They cup their ears to sirens
and cure the ill.
They light a candle for the feast.
Its fire is the flicker
of every word you've told them—
    window, door, listen, arise.

I Found Her

She is a fetus
curled into the womb.
I found her everywhere—
in the dust motes
in the red tendrils
of tired eyes
in the sore paws
of dogs
walking miles
to find better homes
in the *what*
that seemed to be
the stretched skin of my belly
and the taste of sperm
sour and sweet
and yellow with beasts.

She came out of me
jaundiced, and I laid
her on my lap
in the patch
of the April sun.
She was an Aries.
She was fire
but needed more light
so I erased from her
the pain to birth her
and I bathed her

to see through the window
of her eyes.
I potted a handful of pansies
because it still snowed
and I wrote them
while spilling milk
the same color
of that crystal thaw
into a hungry mouth.
I swaddled her
in the blue of lakes.
When there was nothing
left to say
I sang her a lullaby
of old songs
and I bid her to sleep.
Her nocturne sounded
like it would be her last.

She found her way
to all the crooked legs
we carry beneath us to kneel.
It is dark now
and the woods as deep
as homes I've never seen.
I saw her handing them
candles for when
the lights burn out.
I saw her weaving oblivion

like neurons,
strands of flames and smoke
smelling like pine and feathers.

Wings, too,
when she had a chance
to preen
and tell their story.

My Girlfriends

They have hips
made of sugar
with feet of roots
and a piercing light
in their third eye.
They trap mice
in homes built for them
and every child
they may or may not
drop from them
and they hold the world
in their hands
like marbles for a game
they will surely win.

My girlfriends invent gardens
and echo forgiveness
from a god living behind
his cage of stars.
They grasp diminishing light
and let it leave behind
a future the men calculated.
My girlfriends know
the future is in the cards
and the cards are royalty
and no one will bury them
without a grail of gold.

My girlfriends are vixen and deer,
viper and hound.
They live in the wild wood
of incarnation,
in their cave
where the light of fire shines,
the shadows dance
where nothing is illusion,
and silhouettes come to life.

They are birds
and the picture of birds,
hope and the rope
of arms that bind it,
fallen rings behind good ash,
a fathomless song in the dark.

About

Kika Dorsey is an author in Boulder, Colorado. She has a PhD in Comparative Literature and her books include the poetry collections *Beside Herself, Rust, Coming Up for Air, Occupied: Vienna is a Broken Man* and *Daughter of Hunger*, which won the Colorado Authors' League Award for best poetry collection, and the novel *As Joan Approaches Infinity,* a finalist for the Colorado Authors League Award. She has been nominated numerous times for the Pushcart Prize and for Best of Net. Currently, she is a lecturer at the University of Colorado in literature and creative writing. When not teaching or writing, she swims miles in pools and runs and hikes in the open space of Colorado's mountains and plains.

Praise for *Good Ash*

"Threaded through with memories and dreams that articulate the complexity of the human psyche, Kika Dorsey's *Good Ash* reminds me that even as our children cut themselves loose and our parents cross over—as our lives become complicated by our intimate, domestic griefs—'the breath of a day lends wind to the blackbird wings' and 'the desert is an open skirt weaving blossoms above needles.' Dorsey communicates with deft, lyrical imagery an absolute truth I needed to hear again: nature is constant and nature is change, and we can derive comfort from its predictable, variable exquisiteness, even as we negotiate inevitable rites of passage we have no power to prevent. *Good Ash* admits that, yes, to live is to suffer, but it's worth remembering how 'the pond's filthy algae feed[s] the ducks.'"

—Sonia Greenfield, author of *Helen of Troy is High AF*

"Kika Dorsey remains one of the best poets writing today and has deserved wider recognition for years. Her confessional style may be influenced by Plath and Sexton, but make no mistake about it: her voice is uniquely her own. Her language is replete with surprise and revelation, her images brilliant and indelible. In this latest collection of poetry, Dorsey has given us beauty for Good Ash."

—James Cherry, author of *Between Chance and Mercy*

"Kika Dorsey's *Good Ash* had me putting on my sweater believing I was cold and then realizing it was goosebumps from the line-by-line beauty her poems rained down on my spine-tingled soul. Dorsey's honesty is electric and raw, shocks us to our core, and makes us reconsider our definitions of the sublime. These poems unflinchingly interrogate loss and motherhood, the cycle of birth and death, ash and promise. Everything's at stake—her father's suicide haunts, her mother's dementia enervates, her endless efforts to give her children everything consume. 'I reach to touch my shoulders, ache for wings,' she divulges, hunting and descending and lusting to fly all at once. I marveled at the way Dorsey portrays our ancestors as piecing us together from pain in the hopes of a better tomorrow: 'You are behind me like a twisted road and reach before me / like an invisible season,' she tells them, gratefully. And while her 'father's suicide resides / in the ladder of [her] ribs where he climbs and jumps headfirst again and again,' her love for her children emerges from her ever-breaking heart, reminds us of what is possible."

—Elizabeth Strauss Friedman, author of *The Lost Positive*

I know little of healing. I do not even know why my father's
    suicide resides
in the ladder of my ribs where he climbs and jumps headfirst
    again and again.

You see, life is hard and there are different kinds of battles. I
    believe love
can be as solid as bone.

"Simultaneously grounded and in flight, the poems in Good Ash speak to us from landscapes both internal and external. Bone and blood, ghost and grave achieve their songs in the poet's voice: 'I have pinned to the wind every ghost that haunts me.' In describing loved ones' fates, both accidental and intentional, Dorsey's language despairs and longs, celebrates and loves: '… what we unbury / can fly.' These poems confide in us their secrets, share the taste of ashes, show how being in love with the world is a physical, sensory experience. 'I was trying to evolve, / tasting bone.' They will stay with readers long after reading them."

—Jessica Purdy, author of *The Adorable Knife: Poems after The Nutshell Studies of Unexplained Death by Frances Glessner Lee*